CW00506125

Just thinking . . .

Meeting
God
in the
everyday

Julian Hamilton

kevin
mayhew

First published in 2003 by
KEVIN MAYHEW LTD
Buxhall, Stowmarket, Suffolk, IP14 3BW
E-mail: info@kevinmayhewltd.com

KINGSGATE PUBLISHING INC
1000 Pannell Street, Suite G, Columbia, MO 65201
E-mail: sales@kingsgatepublishing.com

9 8 7 6 5 4 3 2 1 0

ISBN 1 84417 059 4
Catalogue No. 1500582

Illustrated by Mike Toner
Cover design by Angela Selfe
Edited and typeset by Elisabeth Bates
Printed and bound in Great Britain

Contents

Introduction   5

Foreword   7

Just thinking, God . . .   9

Prayer for the memory   11

A morning prayer – 1   13

A prayer after reading the temptations   15

Prayer for somebody in pain – 1   17

Prayer for your touch   19

Sometimes, Lord . . .   21

Amazing grace?   23

Ahemmm . . .   25

A morning prayer – 2   27

Honest prayer   29

Prayer for somebody in pain – 2   31

Thank you   33

Ta for the Bible, Lord   35

A morning prayer – 3   37

Prayer for somebody in pain – 3   39

Honestly, Lord   41

Prayer in pain   43

Rock and roll?   45

In the shadows   47

All yours . . .   49

A morning prayer – 4   51

Thanks for good things   53

It's my birthday, Lord   55

I want to see the good stuff, Lord   57

Good stuff of life   59

Thanks   61

Prayer in anger   63

Prayer for sleep   65
Teach me, Lord   67
You are . . .   69
Still searching   71
Shield me   73
Make it real   75
Live in my eyes, Lord   77
I got lost   79
My help comes from God   81
I'm not sure . . .   83
When friends let you down   85
Let's talk   87
Thanks for friends   89
Happy to walk   91
Being bored   93
Wow, Lord!   95

Dedicated to Ceri.
May you learn to pray a lot better than I.

Introduction

It's happening everywhere. Tony Campolo travels the world and preaches. He wakes up every morning and lets Jesus love him - he feels the presence of the living Lord. Scholars and historians point to a western society (that we live in) aching to know the reality of God's presence in their day-to-day existence. My mate, big Charlie, is writing a series of talks to young people inviting them to engage their spirits with the Spirit of God. 'Delirious?' have sung it: 'I wanna go Deeper.' More and more, a ritualistic, traditional, non-engagement faith is on its last legs.

This book of reflections and prayers will probably not rejuvenate your prayer life. It will not become the quintessential tool for the quiet time. It will not provide deep insight, it will not answer any problems you have communicating with the Almighty.

In John 4, Jesus tells a woman he has bumped into that God is Spirit, and those who worship must do so in spirit and truth. This book, I hope, will help you worship truthfully in spirit. So that you will feel and know the difference.

Why?

Because that's how it was written. Honestly.

Use these thoughts as you will. May something of the living God reveal something of the Spirit of truth to the something of your walk with God.

Foreword

When I was young things were easier to understand. I was at the end of that breed of human beings who received their world-view through the objective side of their brain. Tell me something and I could sieve it and agree to agree or disagree with your truth. As Neil Postman pointed out in his book 'Amusing Ourselves To Death', those who live in an image-dominated world exercise the subjective side of their brain much more often and therefore, when telling those who do not remember the first television coming into their home, your truth has limited results. They need to experience it. The word needs to be made flesh much as Jesus originally intended anyway.

Julian Hamilton is a man whose faith and writing is very much alive and very much earthed. In 'Just Thinking...' he makes issues of faith come alive and earths the truths of Scripture. Ideas of Jesus and the following of him get skin and fun and struggle and tears and laughter. Through these prayers, meditations and thoughts once seamless religious definitions can be lived in. You can stretch yourself out and taste and feel and smell the land of the kingdom. Thoughts on God, earthed. And as we said, that is much as Jesus originally intended.

So then, flick open a page and experience the kingdom...

Steve Stockman

Just thinking, God . . .

I was just wondering –
   what's it like being God?
Is there a select committee to help?
The Cabinet, the Executive, the inner advisors?
Or does all the blame for everything
   come onto your shoulders?

Do we blame you for everything,
   all the time?
And is that frustrating, Lord?

Do you wish we could get it
   more right than we do?
Why will you not make us do that?

It must be hard
   standing back – not being heard.
But that choice thing – your decision!

Was that the hardest decision, God?
Giving me free will?
You must have seen what I would do with it.

But I can't see any other way.
Maybe you could not either?
And so that's how it is.

And that's your decision
   and you stick to it.
My God,
   that's love.

Prayer for the memory

When the good times roll
  and my cup overflows,
   Lord, keep me thankful.

When all is fine
  and I have nothing but time,
   Lord, keep me thankful.

When I don't see too well
  but I don't really care,
   Lord, keep me thankful.

When the harvest is here
  and everything is clear,
   Lord, keep me thankful.

When it all makes sense
  and I'm full of confidence,
   Lord, keep me thankful.

When there's nothing but cheer
  and I know you are near,
Lord, keep me thankful.

Thank you, Lord,
  for everything.
Let it be.

A morning prayer.

A morning prayer – 1

Today and every day, Lord,
   let me show your love.
Today and every day,
   let me know your love.

Today and every day,
   let me hold your hand.
Today and every day,
   let me hold somebody else's hand.

Today and every day,
   let me seek to know you more.
Today and every day
   let me know one of your people better.

Today and every day,
   I'm trying to walk with you.
Today and every day,
   keep me travelling, learning, loving.
Because I am yours,
   you are mine.
Let it be
   now and for ever.

A prayer after reading the temptations

To be in your presence –
   that really is my desire.
To know your touch
   deep, deep within.
Because your love takes me higher
   when all is said and done,
   and I sit, more or less alone.
To know your smile
   and experience your peace –
   that's what I want.

I'll always believe it, more or less,
   as different days go by,
   but there are big questions –
   of life, of love, of hope.
I know I'm good at asking
   but not always so good at listening,
   and of course, I could be wrong.
All the tempter asked
   was to do what came naturally,
   and that must have been tempting, really tempting.

Just a quick bit of power
   to make a point,
   remember who you are,
get it all wrapped up.

Oops – I've tried to get you to do that!
Is it still as tempting?

Prayer for someone in Paris ;

Prayer for somebody in pain - 1

I'm down, Lord,
   I'm not sure where.
A lot of people have been telling me where they think I am,
   but I'm not sure if they are right.
I know where I think I am.
I'm in a pit.
And I can't seem to get out just now.

It's dark, Lord.

I'm glad you're here.

I'm not quite at the bottom of the pit,
   but I think I can see it just a bit further down.
It's not a good place.
And it scares me.

I suppose Joseph went through this, then.
Thrown into a pit,
   rather than just stumbling in.

That must have been really horrible,
   but he did get out.
And things did get better,
   and he was healed.

I'm looking up for you to do that again, Lord.
Here I am,
   save me.

Prayer for your trach.

Prayer for your touch

Breathe on me,
    breath of God.
Go on!

Keep breathing,
    gently – like a whisper,
    a whisper that flows through me,
head to toe!

Keep breathing,
    lovingly – like a kiss,
    a kiss that tingles my toes,
    given with love.

Keep breathing,
    steadily – like a breeze,
    a breeze that ruffles my hair,
    filled with freshness.

Breathe on me,
breath of God.
Go on!

Sometimes, Lord . . .

Sometimes, when I hear someone cry,
  sometimes, when I find beauty,
  then
  I see you smile.

Sometimes, when my heart skips a beat,
  sometimes, when your call is loud and clear,
  then
  I see you smile.

Sometimes, when what was hopeless is no longer hopeless,
  sometimes, when I least expect it,
  then
  I see you smile.

Sometimes, when I lose my sense of direction,
  sometimes, when I search for your steps,
  then
  I see you smile.

Sometimes, when I listen to waves against a shore,
  sometimes, when I watch the sun go down,
  then
  I see you smile.

Sometimes, when I look into the eyes of others,
  sometimes, when I look deep into my own eyes,
  then
  I see you smile,
  sometimes.
Thank you.

Amazing grace?

A world where millions suffer,
   while I eat plenty.
A world where few
   control the lives of many.
A world where children die
   because mum and dad left them on a corner.

Amazing grace?

Lives torn apart by bullets.
Lives torn apart by hatred.
Lives torn apart by jealousy.

Amazing grace?

People lie to receive.
People work to simply survive.
People give up, because keeping on is too hard.

Amazing grace?

Yes.

Because what other God would stick around?

I was blind,
   now
   I think I see
   and that's amazing.

Thank you for being amazing
   and giving your grace.

Ahemmmm...

Ahemmm . . .

Dear God,
   I've got a WWJD? thing on.
Could you not just show me?
Ta.

P.S. What bracelet would you wear?

A morning prayer

A morning prayer – 2

It's another morning, Lord,
   thank you for it.
Sun seems to be shining,
   thank you for that, too.
Ahead of me, Lord,
   is a day that could contain anything –
   work to be done,
   people to talk to,
   tasks to complete
   and a desire to get it all done.

Be in today, Lord –
   the work,
   the talking,
   the completing,
   the desiring.
Be in it all –
   make it your day.

Then I can lay my head down tonight
   and smile.
Thank you.

Honest prayer.

Honest prayer

I like to be challenged, Lord,
  and my goodness –
  you challenged people while you were here!

In the synagogue
  you really made them mad!
What were their faces like, Lord?
Did they recognise you
  as the local boy made good?
Or did they still expect you to come home
  and do some carpentry stuff?

Wow – you really blew expectations then!
Telling them you were there for those outside,
  like, completely outside –
  poor people, non-Jewish people, sick people
  and many others,
  others that those 'in' didn't like.

I suppose there's a challenge there, Lord.
A challenge to me – not just to those you spoke to then!
A challenge to listen more honestly
  because you speak the truth
  even when it hurts.

I'll learn to listen, Lord,
  and I'll try not to react the way
  they did in the synagogue!
I'll try to listen
  with my ears open,
  really open.

Prayer for somebody in pain – 2

I could get angry, Lord,
   because I'm in pain here.

I know what's happening to my body,
   many good people have told me.
And I believe them,
   because they wear coats and have clipboards.

But they can't see the inside.
The torment.
And they can give pills,
   but that does not cure the mind,
   because I think the pain will come back.

But I know a way it can become bearable, Lord.
If you sit with me.

So stay a while
   and bring a couple of extra angels to help me.
Because I know you understand about pain
   and I know there are some who suffer more than me.
But just here,
   just now,
   I need a little extra touch.

Thank you

For traces of you
  in the street,
  thank you.

For traces of you
  in people I meet,
  thank you.

For all I can see
  that those who are blind cannot,
  thank you.

For things I can do
that others cannot,
  thank you.

I'm blessed
  and sometimes I forget.
I want to remember all the time
  the things I have.
Because you've given me so much.

And when I'm acting
  like a spoilt child
  next time,
  I'll remember
  all I have.

Most of all –
  thank you
  that I have you.

Ta for the Bible, Lord

What a book, Lord,
   history,
   stories,
   poems,
   dreams,
   tears and laughter,
   song and prayer.

It's a manual for living
   and an answer-book for questions.
An inspiration for tomorrow,
   a reminder of yesterday.

From the stuff I understand
   to difficult passages
   which I haven't a clue about.
From gory, messy things
   to kings and angels.
From places I've never heard of
   to mountain tops of grace,
I love your word.

Let it sink into me
   and make a
   difference
   in my own life story.

A morning page—

A morning prayer - 3

Another morning, Lord,
   another new day.
It would be good to lie down tonight
   knowing something new.
Walk with me today, Lord,
   teach me something
   about someone
   or some place
   that makes me grow in understanding.
Let me see your kingdom
   in a bigger way
   because of today.
I'm searching, Lord,
   and I'm walking,
   holding your hand.

Let's go.

Prayer for somebody in pain !!

Prayer for somebody in pain - 3

It started small, and I could manage it, Lord.
But things seem to have got a lot worse lately.
I have felt angry, bitter, resentful, confused and lonely.
And all around there are those I do know,
but at the minute they are strangers.
Because I know people say they understand
   what I'm going through,
   and I've met some who really do,
   and I love them,
   I cherish them,
   and I thank you for sending them to me.

But now, just between you and me,
   I'm really upset.
Because I don't understand why people suffer -
   least of all me.
And I understand that you hold the big picture,
   the final composition,
   the eternal building plan,
   but I know I'd like to see it right about now,
   so I could understand and see a bit more clearly.
Then I might be able to sit and take what is happening.

So please reveal some things, Lord.
In your eternal wisdom
   give a little glimpse
   of
   'why.'

Honestly, Lord

I was singing in church, Lord,
  something like this –
  'Take my life and let it be
  ever only, all for thee'.

I think I meant it, Lord,
  but it's difficult,
  difficult at the best of times,
  never mind most of the time!
  But I was really surprised, Lord,
  everyone else sang it too!
  So they must all have meant it!

That's really great
  because we can be a great Church then.
Caring,
  showing,
  no back-stabbing, no complaining,
  we young 'uns will feel respected and loved,
  and we will love the older people
  for their patience and wisdom.

Because if we all mean what we say,
  that's going to be it, Lord – isn't it?
Love over all
  'cos that's your way.
Next week then, Lord?

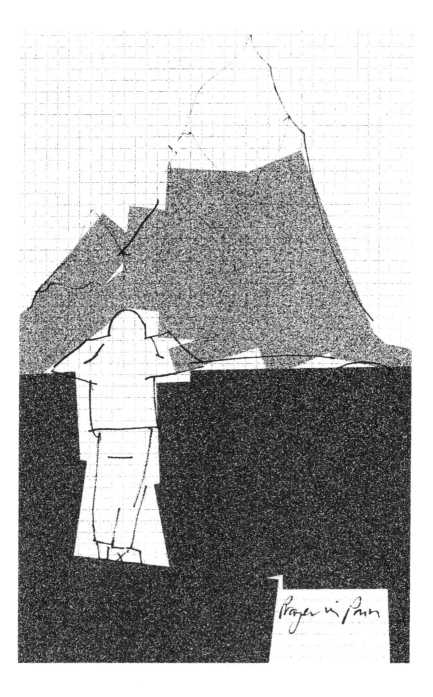

Prayer in Porn

Prayer in pain
(kinda based on Ezekiel 37)

From the depths of the valleys
  it's hard to see, God.
I'm looking up and I see the mountaintop
  but it's a long way off
  and there are rocks along the way.

It can get dark down here.
I have the gear to climb, but it seems to weigh me down.
Do I have too much, God?
Is there something I can leave?

Because I want to climb, Lord – closer, nearer to you.
Stand on the mountain and see the great view,
  breathe deeply with satisfied breaths,
  breaths of completion.
Be happy at what I've done,
  see how far I've come.
I don't want to stay here –
  shadows,
  small animals,
  lots of mud,
  and it's eerily quiet, Lord,
  kinda freaky.

And add to that,
  a load of bones – dead, dry, horrible bones.
It's not a nice place,
  I don't like the bones –
  it's just like they're . . .
  well, dead.

Rock and roll?

I love to dance, Lord,
   to laugh and smile and sing.
You put these things there,
   I'm sure of it.

And I'm also sure
   you put them there
   for a good reason.
Indeed, for a very good reason.
The reason of release –
   a release from tiredness and sameness,
   because when I laugh and smile and sing,
   I'm closer to you.

Closer to your heaven –
a real builder of your Kingdom.
I can do things,
my heart can be a joy.

Explain this, Lord.
If that's true for me,
is it true for your other children?
Because I don't see too much of it, Lord.

Sorry,
   I'm still looking
and sticking with those I find who laugh and dance,
   smile and sing.

IN THE SHADOWS.

In the shadows

What can you see, Lord,
    in the dark?
When we all go to bed
    and the landing light is off?

Do you go to the other side of the world
    when the sun shines?
Do angels stay guard while you work?
How come you can do both – if that's what you do?
Be in the light
    and in the darkness
    at the same time?

As usual, big questions leave me with wonder –
    wonder that you manage,
    because in the daylight
    I can sometimes catch a glimpse of your work,
    but in the darkness?
In the darkness I need to trust –
    I close my eyes.
It's dark –
    I open them,
it's dark.
In the shadows...
You.
Thank you for your protection while I sleep.
Thank you.

All Yours

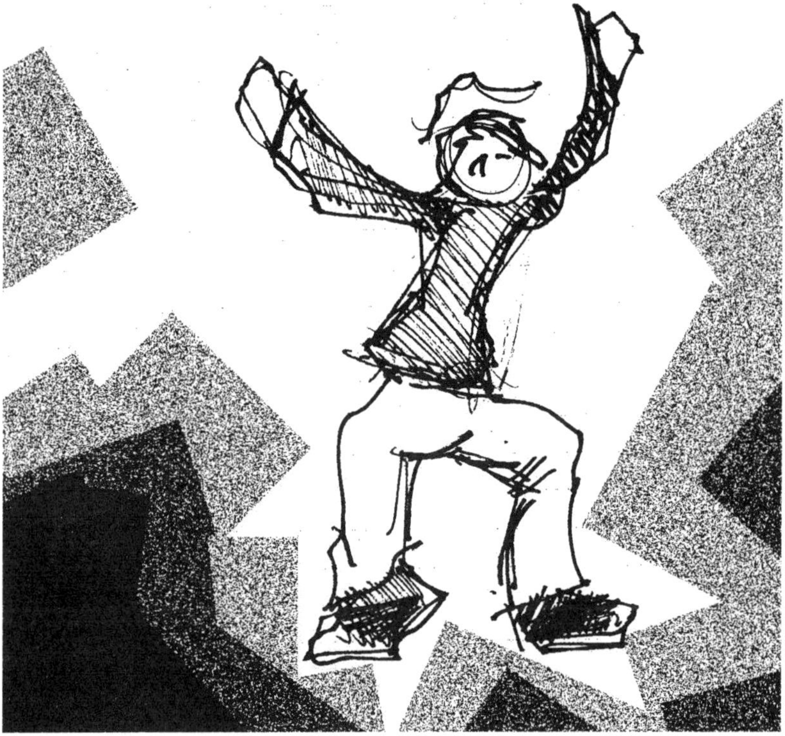

All yours . . .

Up and above,
   round and about,
   here and there,
   simply everywhere.

In and out,
   in the scream and the shout,
   you simply are.
What's it about?
Maybe this,
   inside my mind,
   inside my soul.

Taking control
   inside my life.

So take it all,
   you know it already.
Mend, mould and shape,
   I'm tired of the parts that are fake.

Over to you –
   I'm all here.
All that I am, have and desire,
   in your hands – lift me higher,
   please.

A attending people

A morning prayer – 4

If I see someone today, Lord,
   who needs an extra minute,
   or if I see someone
   who looks sad;
   if I know something good
   that someone else needs to know,
   or if there is something I know
   I should not say;
   if I see somewhere I could help
   or I'm somewhere I should not stay;
   if I know I can make someone feel better
   or think that I can make a small difference,
   help me bring you to these situations,
   and let you in.
Thank you, Lord,
   here we go.

Thanks for good things

You are a mighty God.
You have to be to make me laugh.
I mean, sometimes it is difficult, Lord.

I was in church recently,
and they didn't seem to want to laugh.
Actually, they did not seem to want to smile.
It was all very serious.

Did you wear a serious frown when you listened?

(Excuse me for being rude – did you listen?)

But when I left, I saw a thing that made me laugh.
A young mother was trying to get her toddler to come home,
    and the toddler did not want to come.
It was funny, Lord,
    she teased the child,
    ordered the child,
    pulled the child.
Eventually she pleaded with the child
    and then she lifted the child in her arms,
    and the child laughed
    and settled her head onto her mother's shoulder.

And I laughed.
Can I settle my head onto your shoulder?

Its my Birthday

It's my birthday, Lord

It's my birthday, Lord, and I'm happy.
I'd like to say thank you for putting me here.
And I'd like to say, it's a great world you made.

It's my birthday and I'm feeling older.
And I'd like to thank you for giving me a little more wisdom
    this past year,
    (but not too much at once— next year, Lord, OK?)

It's my birthday and I'm going to celebrate it.
And can you smile at my celebration too, Lord?

It's my birthday and friends have given me presents.
And I like presents – thanks a lot for that idea.

It's my birthday and I'm feeling the centre of attention.
And once in a while it's nice feeling that special kind of love.

It's my birthday and I'm remembering where I've come from.
And I'm glad I can see the steps
    where you've been walking with me.

It's my birthday and I'm just a little nervous
    about a whole new year ahead.
And please, will you be sure and come too.

Thanks, Lord.

I want to see the good stuff, Lord

I want to see the good stuff, Lord,
   the stuff of dreams.
The things that you have put here
   and you want me to discover.

I want to smell the roses
   and all the other great smells.
I want to taste the best of what you've made
   and enjoy the senses you've given me.

I want to smile,
   to know your pleasure,
   to feel the breath of life.
I'm listening, Lord,
   to hear your chuckle,
   sense your smile,
   and join with the clapping of your hands.
Maybe a joke?
Maybe something silly I say?
Maybe a line from a play one of your children wrote?

Whatever it is, Lord,
   that makes you smile,
   I'm searching for it,
   to make me smile also.
So we can laugh together.

Good stuff of life

I want to thank you, Lord,
   for the things that make me smile.
Because I've noticed in this world, Lord,
   there are a lot of things that don't.

I've listened to horrible things on TV,
   things that happen and kill thousands of people.
I've read some nasty stories,
   where children end up hurting for life.
I have some friends in real pain just now,
   and I know a lot of people who are really confused.

So, knowing that you are in all of that,
   and knowing how much you love your world,
I just want to say again, thanks for smiles.
Because they can help me through certain days.
You have made some very funny people,
   and they make me laugh.
Thank you for them.

But it's not just laughter, Lord,
   it's all deeper than that.
Because real joy isn't just a feeling
   or a smile or laughter.
It's knowing you are there in all the stuff of life.
As you cry when we cry,
   teach us to know your joy when we are happy,
   not just on our faces but in our deepest selves.

Take me to a place of joy,
   deep in your kingdom,
   and in my soul.

Thanks

Chocolate in its many forms,
   thanks, Lord.
Friends – their support, love, humour and fun,
   cheers for them as well.
Sunny days,
   and walking barefoot on the beach.
Rocks to climb on top of,
   and streams to paddle through,
   trees to climb, and hide behind.
Footballs to kick around.
Music to sing, to play, to dance to.
Funny stories.
Great TV programmes.
Photographs of times long gone,
   letters of times to come.
Promises of hope,
   words of encouragement.
Colourful food,
   and a nice drink to go with it.
Books to read.
Streets to walk down.
Shops to go into.
A house to live in.
People to talk to.
Stuff to learn.

Just a few things to thank you for, Lord.

Oh, and one more.
The fact that I got up this morning.
Thank you.

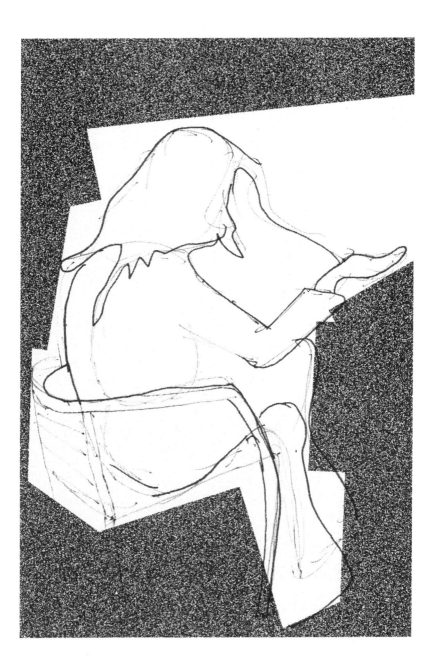

Prayer in anger

I'm not happy, Lord.
Lots of questions,
   lots of frustration,
   lots of confusion,
   and lots of not being satisfied!

Is it OK to be angry, Lord?
Because this situation makes me mad.

I don't know which way to turn,
   I don't know who to talk to.
I'm not sure what to say if anyone asks
   and I'm getting caught up in my own imagination.

Can I change things?
Can I really change things?

Can I change me Lord?

Can you change me Lord?

Cos maybe that's what's really needed here, Lord,
   some change
   in me.
So here I am.
Let's talk . . .

Prayer for sleep

Help me sleep, Lord,

   because I'm tired.

Let me dream, of you,
   and of all you can do . . .

Help me sleep, Lord,

   because I'm tired.

Teach me, Lord

In the evening,
   all the day,
   throughout the night,
   and in every way,
   help me remember,
   trust me to know,
   how much you love me
   and help me to grow.

You teach me your ways,
   you teach me your heart,
I'm listening for more
   with every fresh start.

So here I am, Lord,
   ready for another lesson.
Let's go.

You are . . .

You are the Lord.
You are my might.
You are the truth.
You are my right.

You are the beginning.
You are my friend.
You are the comfort.
You are my end.

You are the healer.
You are my light.
You are the teacher.
You are my delight.

You are the King.
You are my call.
You are the life.
My all in all.

Still searching

If I could know everything, Lord,
   about you and this world;
   if someone told me I could understand everything,
   have no mystery
   and no story untold;
   if I had the chance
   to solve it all,
   know every twist and turn
   and never miss a beat,
   I think I would hesitate,
   stop and think.

Because I love you, Lord,
   and part of the reason why
   is the 'don't know'.
The mist,
   the questions,
   the discovery,
   the adventure.

It's fantastic, Lord.
So I'm searching,
   I'm looking
   and living with eyes wide open
   to see where you will jump out next!

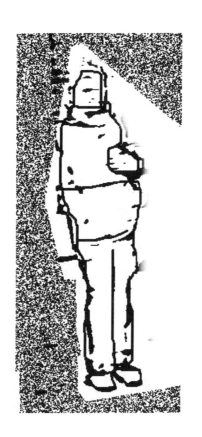

Shield me

Shield me, Lord,
   lots of things come my way.
You know all about them.
Relationships,
   or lack of.
Work,
   or lack of.
Friends,
   or lack of.
Faith,
   or lack of.

Shield me.
Let me have space to breathe.
Space to breathe God-air,
   the very air of life.

Your space, your air, in your light.

Make it real

God,
  I've decided – again –
  I'm walking the story.

I'm going to live it,
  make it real.

Not some easy, half-life,
  put-it-in-a-bottle-get-it-when-need it real
  but really real.

I'm not going to be scared.
But I'm not going to pretend it will be easy.

This is the stuff of freedom,
  this is the stuff of truth,
  and the truth seems to say we are hurting in this world.

So I'm going to help you help us.
I'm travelling after you,
  searching for your clues,
  stepping in the footprints you've left,
  and doing this thing called life.

I'm walking.

Live in my eyes, Lord

I saw a woman, Lord.
She was great.

Really happy,
   carefree,
   smart.
Lived in the noon of the day.
She spread light,
   warmth,
   affection,
   spirit wherever she went.

She inspired me, Jesus,
   because she knew you.
And I knew, she knew you, even before she told me,
   because she was great, Lord.

You were in her eyes.

Thank you for living in people's eyes.
Make a nest, and sparkle through mine.

I got lost

I got lost somewhere, Lord.
Not exactly sure where it was,
   not exactly sure what happened,
   but it all went wrong.
Somehow.

Things were great.
Friends were fantastic.
Family was wonderful.
You were teaching,
I was listening.
But I got lost.

I can't remember the last turn.
I can't remember the final twist in the road.
I just know, somewhere I got lost.

Did you get lost, Jesus?
Did the disciples ever go down a road
   that you were not sure about,
   but you walked with them,
   because they said they had been there before?
Did they ever admit they were lost?
Or did they expect you to click your fingers
   and get them sorted?

I feel a bit stupid God – because now I'm going to ask you
to click your fingers, and get me sorted ...

I'm looking for a sign-post.
I'm looking for you.

My help comes from God

I lift my eyes up . . .
   I look for your help.
I lift my feet,
   I long for your steps to walk in.
I look to the sky,
   I search for traces of you.
I stumble forward, walking aimlessly,
   I stumble for your worn path.

Where does my help come from?
Where will my feet tread?
How do I claim a victory in my life?

My help comes from only one place.
The only place.
The only one.
My help comes from the maker of the sky,
   the layer of the path.
My help comes from God.

I'm not sure

Hmmmmmmm.
I'm not sure, Lord,
   about a lot of things.
I'm not even sure, what I'm not sure about,
   if you understand what I mean?!
I'm not sure about how I look,
   I'm not sure about the effort I put in at school,
   I'm not sure about how good my friends are
   and sometimes I'm not sure if I'm being me or someone stupid!

I'm trying to be like you.
But I'm not 100% sure what you are like!
I'm trying to be good
   but I'm not sure if everything I like is bad.
I'm trying to work it all out . . .

OK, Lord,
   I know there are no easy answers.
But please can I have some of the slightly easier ones,
   today?
As fuel to continue my quest into you!

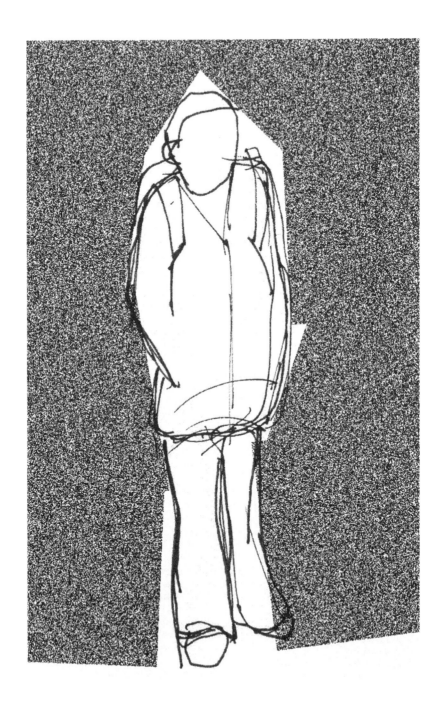

When friends let you down

Excuse me God.
Got something to ask,
  I know you are used to that!
But this time I'm angry.
My friends let me down.
They did some stupid stuff
  and I got mad.
Pretty stupid, eh?
But I don't know what to say,
  I don't know how to say it.
I think if I do anything, it'll make things worse.

So do I need these friends, Lord?
Or do you think I need broader horizons?
Do you want me to be honest
  or live below a blanket of 'pretend'?

I'm well confused.
There are things that need to be said
  but I don't think I can say any of them.

I suppose it's time for you to do a God-special.
Come on, Lord,
  let's see another miracle in my life . . .

Let's talk

Let's sit a while and talk,
   you and I.
Talking is good for the soul,
   it's how I get through the day!
I want to share with you
   lots of me.
I want to tell you about plans,
   about an exciting future,
   about a messed up but forgiven past.
I want to share my dreams,
   my hopes and fears – there are lots of fears,
   my perfect partner,
   my biggest disaster,
   my most wonderful friend,
   my weirdest experience.

Will you listen?
Stay a little while
   then I will listen to you,
   I promise I will listen.

It's good to sit here with you,
   thank you.

Thanks for friends

Cheers, Lord,
    for my friends.
At times they can be hard,
    and I can be a bad friend.

But to be honest,
    I need them – I think you know that.

They bring a love to my life
    that I'm sure comes from you.

They laugh at my gags,
    tell me their stories,
    trust me with their secrets
    and let me be the me you made.

Bless them, God.
Be with them in their everyday.
Especially the ones who are not sure about you
    but don't laugh at me for having you.
Keep them safe,
    listen to their hearts,
    calm their fears
and show them you.

I'm willing to be part of that process, Lord.
Thank you so much for them,
    help me to love them the way you do.

Happy to walk

Here I am again, Lord.

And all is cool.

I'm content to be thinking and talking to you alone
   because you alone are the keeper of all that I am.
You know more about me than I do,
   and your dreams for me are bigger than mine.

I'm happy to walk this path, Lord.
The path of discovery,
   the path of learning about you,
   about life,
   about love,
   about happiness.

I love walking.
Beaches,
   countryside,
   crowded streets,
   empty avenues.

As long as the
   sand is beneath my feet,
   the grass is touching my ankles,
   the pavement has room for me
   and the cobbles lead me forward, not back.

Then I'm happy to walk.
Happy to walk in your path.

Being bored

I'm going to confess, Lord,
   I know this thing should not happen to me
   but it does,
   and so I'll say sorry . . . for being bored.

That's quite a confession, I know,
   especially since you've made such an amazing world.
I mean, the people, the places, it is cool.

But sometimes, just sometimes,
   I'm ready for another adventure,
   or something new to see, or do.
But there seems nothing new to do.
Same people, same places,
   same complaints, same moans.
And I suppose I let that get to me.
So I suppose my prayer, Lord,
   is that you would help me at those times.
Help me to see you hiding everywhere,
   like a big God-hide-and-seek!

I'm sure you have things to teach,
   things for me to realise, people for me to meet.
I suppose, Lord, it's not even all new people and places,
   there are plenty of people and places in my life,
   that maybe I need to see them with your eyes . . .

That would be wicked, Lord, seeing as you do.
Sounds a bit dangerous tho'!
I might start to love everybody and everything!
How scary . . .

Wow, Lord!

Wow, Lord, like . . . wow.
What a planet!
What a wonderful world!
What an amazing creation!
What a creator you are . . .

I can't contain myself.
I just want to jump,
   to shout,
   to sing,
   to laugh,
   to punch the air,
   to delight in your work.

The sun,
   the sea,
   the birds,
   the fresh air,
   the freedom in your creation,
   the love in the gentle touch of your hand,
   the print of your finger,
   the signs of where you have walked.

It's great, Lord – really great.
Can I have a view in heaven that reminds me of this earth?

Maybe that's it, Lord . . .
Maybe that's why you made it so lovely . . .
So we can have a little glimpse of what's coming?
Wow, Lord – if things here can be beautiful
My wee mind won't be able to handle heaven!!!
Mind you – I'll take the risk in wanting to come anyway, Lord!